The British Prime Minister Quiz Book

By

Joanne Hayle

Questions: The 1700's to 1829.

Today, we have the Conservative Party and the Labour Party as Britain's two main political factions vying for votes. Which two parties were operating in the 1700's?

Tory and Labour.
Whig and Tory.
Whig and Liberal.

Both party names were originally used by people as insulting terms. Whig was short for *whiggamor,* a Scottish word. What was a whiggamor?

Sheep farmer.
Cattle driver.
Chicken breeder.

What was a Tory, from the Irish word *Toraidhe?* Also called Abhorrers, these figures were supporters of King Charles II when he chose to dissolve parliament in 1679 and they abhorred the petitions being signed to recall parliament.

An outlaw or robber.

A coward.

A lame horse.

Who is widely considered to be the first British Prime Minister?

Sir Robert Walpole.

William Cavendish, Duke of Devonshire.

William Pitt The Elder.

Was the first Prime Minister a Whig or a Tory?

Whig.

Tory.

Neither.

Sir Robert Walpole.

Which monarch did Sir Robert Walpole serve as Prime Minister from 1721 until deposed in 1742?

George I.

George II.

George III.

Sir George Villiers, High Sheriff of Leicestershire (circa 1544-1606) was the father of George Villiers, 1st Duke of Buckingham, a favourite of King James I (VI of Scotland.) Sir George was an ancestor to how many British Prime Ministers, including David Cameron and Sir Winston Churchill?

8.

16.

25.

Who is the longest serving Prime Minister in British history?

Sir Robert Walpole.

William Cavendish, Duke of Devonshire.

Sir Winston Churchill.

Who was the first Prime Minister to live at 10 Downing Street?

Sir Robert Walpole.

William Gladstone.

Benjamin Disraeli.

In which year did he move in to 10 Downing Street?

1735.

1841.

1903.

At that time, 10 Downing Street was officially called the residence of the whom – Another title held by the person we call Prime Minister?

First Lord of the Treasury.

First Lord of the Realm.

First Minister's House.

The country's 2nd Prime Minister was a Whig named Spencer Compton, Earl of Wilmington. His tenure was short. Why?

He was universally despised.

He died in office.

He switched parties and became a Tory.

To which Member of Parliament, in his own party, was Compton speaking when he said: "Sir, you have a right to speak, but the House has a right to judge whether they will hear you."

Sir Robert Walpole.

William Pitt the Elder.

Thomas Pelham-Holles, Duke of Newcastle Upon Tyne.

The 3rd British Prime Minister was Henry Pelham, another Whig and an admirer of Walpole's skills. What relation was he to the 4th Prime Minister, Thomas Pelham-Holles, Duke of Newcastle Upon Tyne?

Elder brother.

Father.

Younger brother.

Why did Henry Pelham's tenure as Prime Minister last just 7 months from August 1743?

Thomas Pelham-Holles staged a coup.

Henry died.

Henry resigned because he hated the role.

Thomas Pelham-Holles, Duke of Newcastle upon Tyne.

Which role had Thomas Pelham-Holles held for over 30 years before his time as Prime Minister began?

Speaker of the House.
Lord High Admiral.
Secretary of State.

How many terms did this Duke of Newcastle upon Tyne spend as Prime Minister?

2.

3.

5.

What was Pelham-Holles' nickname?

Hubble-bubble.

Hells-Pelles.

Coals to Newcastle.

Which Prime Minister negotiated peace to end the 1756-1763 pan-European and colonial Seven Years War?

John Stuart, 3rd Earl of Bute.

William Pitt the Elder.

Sir Robert Peel.

What role had John Stuart, 3rd Earl of Bute held prior to his selection as the first ever Tory Prime Minister?

Secretary of State.

Tutor to Prince George, the future King George III.

Chancellor of the Exchequer.

To decrease national debt, for which drink did Bute introduce a tax in 1763 of 4 shillings per hogshead? The tax caused riots and his resignation from office?

Gin.

Beer.

Cider.

His successor, George Grenville, ensured that the above unpopular tax was applied. What else did George Grenville achieve in 1765?

He introduced a stabling tax for horses that the gentry owned.

He introduced a stamp tax for mail in the US colonies.

He reduced politicians' wages.

Grenville was dismissed by King George III in 1766. However, the Whigs remained in power under the 2nd Marquess of Rockingham. What was his name?

Charles Watson-Wentworth.
John Spencer-Churchill.
William Cavendish-Bentinck.

2nd Marquess of Rockingham.

William Pitt the Elder rose to power in 1766; what is he credited with the creation of?

Free speech for all.
The British Empire.
Global diplomatic channels.

Which nickname did he earn?

The Great Liberator.
The Great Commoner.
The Great Orator.

Who did William Pitt the Elder marry on 16th November 1754?

Hester Grenville, future Prime Minister George Grenville's sister.
 Lady Charlotte Cavendish-Bentinck, the daughter of the 3rd Earl of Portland; British Prime Minister twice.
Lady Mary Stuart, sister of Prime Minister John Stuart, 3rd Earl of Bute.

Scandalous Prime Minister, Augustus Henry Fitzroy, the 3rd Duke of Grafton owed his political survival to what major factor?

His wife Anne's affair, pregnancy by her lover and remarriage post-divorce surpassed his misdemeanours in the electorate's opinion.
The popular William Pitt the Elder's support kept him in office.
His exemplary military record made the public more forgiving of his loose morals.

Which Tory was Prime Minister when America gained independence from British rule?

Spencer Perceval.
William Addington, Viscount Sidmouth.
Lord Frederick North.

For how many years was this man the Prime Minister of Britain? (Although he is remembered unfavourably as the man who "lost" America.)

7.

12.

19.

Whig Prime Minister William Petty served in 1782-1783. Which aristocratic titles did Petty hold?

2nd Earl of Shelburne. 1st Marquess of Lansdowne.
2nd Earl of Liverpool, Baron Hawkesbury.
4th Earl of Bute, Lord Mount Stuart.

William Petty's successor said: "My fears are not that the attempt to perform this duty will shorten my life, but that I shall neither bodily nor mentally perform it as I should." Who was he?

William Pitt the Elder.
William Cavendish-Bentinck, Duke of Portland.
William Pitt the Younger.

Who delivered the country's first Budget speech in April 1802? The budget was and still is the financial plan of the government laid out in a statement.

William Pitt the Elder.

Henry Addington, Viscount Sidmouth.

Augustus Fitzroy, 3rd Duke of Grafton.

William Pitt the Younger is the youngest Prime Minister in British history. How old was he when he became Prime Minister?

24.

28.

32.

How old was Pitt The Younger when he died?

46.

66.

86.

He oversaw the Act of Union in 1800. What did this act involve?

It united Great Britain with newly acquired colonies.

It united Great Britain with European mainland powers.

It united Great Britain with Ireland.

How old was William Pitt the Elder when he passed away in 1778?

69.

76.

96.

Prime Minister Henry Addington's father acted in what capacity to William Pitt the Elder?

Secretary of State.

Private Secretary.

Physician.

Which early 19th century Prime Minister said this? "In youth, the absence of pleasure is pain, in old age the absence of pain is pleasure."

William Cavendish-Bentinck, Duke of Portland.

Henry Addington, Viscount Sidmouth.

George Canning.

What was Henry Addington's nickname?

The Doctor.
The Grim Reaper.
The Pickpocket.

William Wyndham Grenville was the son of George Grenville, Prime Minister 1763-1765. Although William Grenville resigned as Prime Minister in 1807 after only approximately 13 months, what act is he credited with?

The abolition of slavery overseas in the British Empire.
Introducing a minimum working wage in Britain.
Informing the hedonistic Prince Regent (later King George IV) that he could expect no political support for a petition asking for a raised personal income.

William Grenville was married to which of these ladies?

Anne North, daughter of Lord Frederick North.
Anne Pitt, a great niece of William Pitt the Elder.

Anne Liddell, former wife of 3rd Duke of Grafton.

Between 1809-1812 Spencer Perceval was Tory Prime Minister. What ended his political career?

A personal scandal.
Assassination.
A dispute about expenses he'd claimed.

What career did Perceval pursue prior to politics?

Medicine.
Archaeology.
Law.

Who served as British Prime Minister between 1812 and 1827?

Robert Banks-Jenkinson, Earl of Liverpool.
William Pitt the Younger.
Charles Grey, Earl Grey.

At 119 days, the shortest tenure as Prime Minister is held by George Canning, a former Foreign Secretary. He was Prime

Minister between 10th April and 8th August 1827. He believed that "The happiness of constant occupation is infinite." What were his last words as he died of pneumonia?

"Spain and Portugal."
"I shall put my pen down now."
"Who will remember me?"

George Canning.

Canning died at Chiswick House in London, owned by successive Dukes of Devonshire until 1929. Which Whig leader passed away at the property in September 1806?

Henry Fox, Baron Holland.

Charles James Fox.

Henry Fox-Strangeways, 2nd Earl of Ilchester.

Frederick Robinson, Viscount Goderich was Prime Minister from late 1827 in to 1828. Apart from Goody Goderich and Prosperity Robinson, what was his other nickname?

The Blubberer.

The Blusterer.

The Blusher.

Who became Prime Minister after Viscount Goderich's departure?

Arthur Wellesley, The Duke of Wellington.

William Lamb, Lord Melbourne.

Charles Grey, 2nd Earl Grey.

Earl Grey passed the 1832 Reform Act which started over a century of further political reforms. What else is Charles Grey renowned for?

A blend of coffee.

A blend of tea.

A blend of cocoa.

How many terms did Grey serve as Prime Minister?

1.

2.

3.

In which year did the Tory party become the Conservative party?

1834.

1841.

1854.

Who was Prime Minister at the time of the name change, confirmed by the Tamworth Manifesto?

Sir Robert Peel.

Charles Grey, Earl Grey.

Arthur Wellesley, Duke of Wellington.

William IV is reputed to have selected William Lamb, Lord Melbourne to form a government after Earl Grey's resignation because...?

He was able "to silence his critics with his legendary charm."
He was "best known to the common man and no fool."
He was the "least bad choice."

How many terms did Lord Melbourne serve as Prime Minister?

2.

4.

5.

Questions: Queen Victoria's Prime Ministers 1837-1901.

Which royal affectionately called Melbourne "Dear Lord M.?"

Adelaide, William IV's wife.

Queen Victoria.

Prince Albert.

How old was Arthur Wellesley, The Duke of Wellington when he died in 1852?

83.

93.

103.

What was Wellington's nickname?

The Steely Duke.

The Golden Duke.

The Iron Duke.

Where in London is the Wellington Arch situated?

In Hyde Park.
At Wellington Barracks.
The Houses of Parliament.

Arthur Wellesley, 1st Duke of Wellington circa 1844.

"There seem to me to be very few facts, at least ascertainable facts, in politics." Which Prime Minister is quoted as saying this?

Sir Robert Peel.
Lord Melbourne.
Winston Churchill.

Who was Prime Minister for 3 short tenures; in 1852,1858-1859 and 1866-1868?

Edward Stanley Smith, 14th Earl of Derby.
William Gladstone.
Benjamin Disraeli.

George Hamilton Gordon, Earl of Aberdeen was Prime Minister 1852-1855, which poet was he related to?

George Byron.
Percy Bysshe Shelley.
Samuel Taylor Coleridge.

Aberdeen resigned in 1855 because of his perceived failures managing which crisis?

The Crimean War.

The Corn Laws.

The Bedchamber Crisis. (Queen Victoria refused to change her ladies of the bedchamber.)

Henry Temple, Viscount Palmerston, replaced Aberdeen. In 1857 he was instrumental in which of these matters?

Introducing the divorce court in Britain.

Passing the 2nd Reform Act.

Repealing the Corn Laws.

Which of these was one of his nicknames?

Lord Romantic.

Lord Cupid.

Lord Swashbuckler.

Lord John Russell, Prime Minister 1856-1862 and 1866-1867, was the 3rd son of which duke?

6th Duke of Bedford.

4th Duke of Northumberland.

1st Duke of Wellington.

In which year was Benjamin Disraeli "Dizzy" born?

1794.

1804.

1814.

A Prime Minister twice, Disraeli was also an acclaimed what?

Painter.

Writer.

Sculptor.

He is the only British Prime Minister in history to be of which faith?

Judaism.

Hinduism.

Buddhism.

In which year was Disraeli given the title of Earl of Beaconsfield?

1866.

1879.

1881.

Why was this earldom awarded, primarily?

He had succeeded in making Queen Victoria the Empress of India.

He had simply charmed the queen in to bestowing a title on him. He was acknowledged as her favourite Prime Minister.

He retired from politics to concentrate on his other interests.

What was the name of Dizzy's country home located in High Wycombe, Buckinghamshire? Today it is open to the public.

Highclere Castle.

Hughenden Manor.

Hever Castle.

William Gladstone, Queen Victoria's least favourite Prime Minister, held the position how many times during his political career?

2.

3.

4.

Born in Liverpool in 1809, in which year did Gladstone's last tenure as Prime Minister begin?

1852.

1872.

1892.

Where in London was Gladstone buried in 1898? (He died on 19th May at Hawarden Castle in Wales.)

Westminster Abbey.

St. Paul's Cathedral.

Palace of Westminster.

William Ewart Gladstone.

In 1894, the 5th Earl of Rosebery became Prime Minister. What was his name?

Arnold Xavier Rose.

Arthur Arnold Daisy.

Archibald Phillip Primrose.

Which princess of the British royal family did he ask permission to marry?

Princess Mary, daughter of George V and Queen Mary.
Princess Victoria, daughter of Edward VII and Queen Alexandra.
Lady May Cambridge, a niece of George V and Queen Mary.

Why was Rosebery refused permission?

Edward, Prince of Wales and later King Edward VII was opposed to royals marrying political figures.

She declined, saying that she would marry for love alone; not friendship, personal freedom, or a new title.

Queen Victoria was employing her as a private secretary and refused to release her for marriage. Duty first.

This lady was destined not to marry the 5th Earl of Rosebery.

Robert Gascoyne-Cecil, 3rd Marquess of Salisbury was created Prime Minister on three separate occasions. Which renowned figure was he a descendant of?

William Cecil, Lord Burghley, Queen Elizabeth I's long serving chief advisor and Secretary of State.
Charles Grey, Earl Grey, 19th century Prime Minister.
William Laud, Archbishop of Canterbury at the time of Charles I's reign and execution.

What record does the 3rd Marquess of Salisbury hold amongst Prime Ministers?

He was a Conservative, Liberal and Labour party Home Secretary during his career.

He gave the longest speech in the House of Commons.

He was the tallest Prime Minister in British history.

Which educational establishments did the three Prime Ministers between 1880 and 1902 all attend?

Harrow and St. Mary's College, University of St. Andrews.

Eton and Christ Church, Cambridge University.

Eton and Christ Church, Oxford University.

Questions: 20th Century Prime Ministers.

In 1900, Winston Churchill, two time 20th century Conservative Prime Minister, first became a Member of Parliament. For which town did he compete in 1899 and lose before a win in 1900?

Oldham.
Oxford.
Salisbury.

Arthur Balfour replaced the Marquess of Salisbury as Prime Minister in 1902. What relationship did they have?

Balfour was Salisbury's godson.
Salisbury was Balfour's uncle.
Balfour was Salisbury's 1st cousin.

Which renowned philosopher and Prime Minister said: "I am more or less happy when being praised, not very comfortable when being abused, but I have moments of uneasiness when being explained."

Henry Campbell-Bannerman.

Herbert Henry Asquith.

Arthur Balfour.

Henry Campbell-Bannerman became Prime Minister in 1905. Why was history made?

It was the first time a party had won over 80% of the votes in a general election.

It was the first time that the title of Prime Minister was officially used.

It was the first time that a man under the age of 20 had become British Prime Minister.

He died at 10 Downing Street in 1908. What abbreviation was he normally referred to by?

CB.

PMH.

HCB.

Campbell-Bannerman's Chancellor of the Exchequer became the new Prime Minister. Who was he?

Herbert Henry Asquith.

Winston Churchill.

Andrew Bonar Law.

Which Prime Minister is the only one to have served 3 monarchs during their time in office? (George V, Edward VIII and George VI.)

Stanley Baldwin.

Andrew Bonar Law.

David Lloyd George.

In 1925 H.H. Asquith was given the Order of the Garter, the highest chivalric order, and which title?

Earl of Bristol and Asquith.

Earl of Oxford and Asquith.

Earl of Reading and Asquith.

What financial support measure did Asquith implement in 1909? Payment was subject to meeting criteria; including being of "good character."

Child benefit payments for married mothers.

Income support for low earners.

The state pension for the over 70's.

Who succeeded Asquith as Prime Minister on 6th December 1916?

David Lloyd George.

Andrew Bonar Law.

Stanley Baldwin.

H.H. Asquith's son, Anthony, 1902-1968, became known to the public by embracing which profession?

Politics.

Film directing.

Photography.

Prime Minister Andrew Bonar Law instigated which of these to help Britain recover from the First World War?

The Peace Treaty.

The Tranquillity Manifesto.
The Calm Restoring Budget.

How long was Andrew Bonar Law the Prime Minister for?

209 days.
346 days.
471 days.

What did David Lloyd George's fall as Prime Minister result in?

The Liberal Party never formed a government again.
Votes for women.
Prohibition, in common with the USA.

Which Conservative Prime Minister had author and journalist Rudyard Kipling as a cousin?

Winston Churchill.
Stanley Baldwin.
Anthony Eden.

In 1943, aged 80, David Lloyd George caused a scandal by doing what?

He married his secretary (and mistress.)
He criticised George VI.
He called Winston Churchill a fool on live radio. (Known as the wireless.)

Who was the first Labour Party Prime Minister in 1924?

David Lloyd George.
James Ramsay-McDonald.
Clement Attlee.

Ramsay-McDonald was said to have been infatuated with which society and political hostess?

Edith, Marchioness of Londonderry.
Lady Emerald Cunard.
Sibyl, Lady Colefax.

Between 1924-1929, Churchill served in which political office? A colourful character, he had defected to the Liberals in 1904 but returned to the Conservatives (calling himself a Constitutionalist) in the November 1924 general election.

Foreign Secretary.

Chancellor of the Exchequer.

Minister of War.

How many times did Stanley Baldwin serve as Prime Minister?

3.

4.

5.

Which Conservative Prime Minister was faced with Edward VIII's abdication crisis in 1936? He made it clear that Edward could not marry divorcee Wallis Simpson and remain on the throne; the head of the Church of England. (Edward never forgave him.)

Winston Churchill.

Stanley Baldwin.

Anthony Eden.

Which Prime Minister optimistically, and mistakenly, said: "This is the second time in our history that there has come back from Germany to Downing Street peace with honour. I believe it is peace for our time."

Stanley Baldwin.
Neville Chamberlain.
Winston Churchill.

What role did Neville Chamberlain hold before he became Prime Minister?

Chancellor of the Exchequer.
Foreign Secretary.
Home Secretary.

Sir Winston Churchill. (1874-1965.)

Having already won the Nobel Prize for Literature in 1953, what unique honour was bestowed on Sir Winston Churchill by the U.S. Congress on 9th April 1963?

U.S. Citizenship.
Permission to host guests at the White House.
U.S. Medal of Honor.

Clement Attlee and the Labour Party won the first election after World War II. What organisation did his government create? It was officially launched on 5th July 1948?

The British Red Cross.
The National Health Service.
The Office of National Statistics.

Churchill and the Conservatives returned to power in 1951. Between October 1951 and early March 1952 Churchill also served in which office? The new holder of the role had to conclude his duties as Governor General of Canada.

Chancellor of the Exchequer.
Education Minister.
Minister of Defence.

Sir Anthony Eden succeeded Winston Churchill as Prime Minister in 1955; which high profile role in government did he hold for 3 separate terms prior to the top job?

Foreign Secretary.
Home Secretary.
Chancellor of the Exchequer.

Knighted in 1954, Eden was given which earldom in 1961?

Earl of Westminster.
Earl of Avon.
Earl of Abercrombie.

What nickname did Harold MacMillan, the Conservative Prime Minister from 1957-1963, have?

Big Mac.
MacDone.
Supermac.

What did MacMillan tell Queen Elizabeth II when he took on the role of Prime Minister?

That he was the perfect man for the task.
That he thought his government would last less than 6 weeks.
That he had no idea how a half-American publisher's son could be a British Prime Minister.

MacMillan was the last former Prime Minister to be created an Earl in 1984. He became the Earl of Stockton. What rank of honour have later ministers achieved as "life peers?" e.g. Margaret Thatcher and John Major.

Former Prime Ministers have been awarded baronetcies.
Former Prime Ministers hold marquessates.
Former Prime Ministers have been given dukedoms.

Sir Alec Douglas-Home followed Macmillan as Conservative leader and Prime Minister. How long was he Prime Minister for?

363 days.
3 years, 63 days.
8 years, 3 days.

What was unusual about his appointment as Prime Minister?

He was 19 years old at the time.
He was semi-retired and living in France when elected.
He renounced his earldom, and his seat in the House of Lords, to serve as Prime Minister in the House of Commons.

Labour, led by Harold Wilson (1916-1995) won the 1964 election by what majority?

4.

40.

400.

Harold was Wilson's middle name, what was his true first name?

Edward.

George.

James.

Why did Wilson call a general election in 1970?

He was confident that he, and the Labour Party, would win resoundingly.

He wished to retire as Prime Minister.

The public demanded a say in the country's proposed membership of the European Economic Community.

Who became the Prime Minister after the 1970 election?

James Callaghan.
Alec Douglas-Home.
Edward Heath.

What political role did Wilson hold between 1974-1976?

Prime Minister.
Home Secretary.
Culture Minister.

Which Prime Minister suspended the Death Penalty in England, Wales and Scotland?

Harold MacMillan.
James Callaghan.
Harold Wilson.

What was unique about James Callaghan's career?

He only went in to politics three years before becoming Prime Minister. No one expected him to win the Labour party leadership election.

He was the only 20th century Prime Minister to have held the 4 major offices (Prime Minister, Chancellor, Home Secretary and Foreign Secretary.)

He was the great, great, great grandson of Lord Palmerston, Prime Minister at the time of the Crimean War.

What rank did Edward Heath achieve in the British army during the Second World War?

Brigadier.
Lieutenant-Colonel.
Sergeant Major.

Despite both being Conservatives, which future Prime Minister was Heath a high-profile critic of?

James Callaghan.
Margaret Thatcher.
John Major.

During Callaghan's tenure, how high did unemployment rise?

1 million people.
1.5 million people.
2.5 million people.

The May 1979 general election was won by which leader and party?

Margaret Thatcher, Conservatives.
Michael Foot, Labour Party.
David Steel, Liberal Party.

Who was the longest serving 20th century British Prime Minister?

David Lloyd George.
Harold Wilson.
Margaret Thatcher.

When Margaret Thatcher became Conservative Prime Minister, she was the first female Prime Minister in British history. How many females have filled this role since?

0.

1.

2.

Margaret Thatcher's father, Alfred Roberts, had filled which office in Grantham, Lincolnshire?

Liberal Member of Parliament.

Mayor.

Town Cryer.

Margaret Thatcher. 1925-2013.

Source: The Margaret Thatcher Foundation.

What was Margaret Thatcher's nickname?

The Stubborn Lady.

The Old Boot.

The Iron Lady.

What was a major factor in her downfall as Prime Minister?

The introduction of the Poll Tax.
She was a woman in a male dominated environment.
The resignation of her key allies in government.

During the 1990's the Labour Party, led by Tony Blair, rebranded as New Labour. They were said to be influenced by which iconic Prime Minister's visions?

Margaret Thatcher.
Winston Churchill.
Robert Walpole.

Who succeeded Thatcher as Prime Minister on 28th November 1990, holding the office until 2nd May 1997?

John Major.
Tony Blair.
Gordon Brown.

What major role had this man held in Thatcher's last government?

Chancellor of the Exchequer.
Foreign Secretary.
Home Secretary.

At what age did John Major win his first seat as a Conservative councillor for Lambeth Council in London? (Born 1943.)

21.
25.
32.

He won his first parliamentary seat – Huntingdon in Cambridgeshire - in which year?

1975.
1979.
1983.

Questions: Recent History.

Former Labour Prime Minister Gordon Brown holds a doctorate in which subject from Edinburgh University?

Politics.
History.
Religion.

Gordon is his middle name, what is his true Christian name?

James.
Anthony.
Nicholas.

Following Princess Diana's death in 1997, which former Prime Minister was appointed as a special guardian to Princes William and Harry?

Margaret Thatcher.
John Major.
James Callaghan.

Which party was Tony Blair leader of, and later Prime Minister for, from 1994?

Conservatives.
Labour.
Liberal Democrats.

What did Blair announce on 27th June 2007?

His resignation as Prime Minister.
His plan to stand for a record 4th time as Prime Minister.
His decision to leave politics and return to law, his original career.

Blair was the youngest Prime Minister since Lord Liverpool in 1812. How old was Tony Blair when he became Prime Minister?

28.
37.
43.

Who succeeded Tony Blair as part of a private deal they had probably agreed in 1994?

Neil Kinnock.
Gordon Brown.
Margaret Beckett.

What are former Conservative Prime Minister David Cameron's middle names?

William Donald.
Hugh Alistair.
Lucian James.

Which Conservative politician from Sir Winston Churchill's era is David Cameron related to? You can see the resemblance.

Sir Alfred Duff Cooper.
Sir Anthony Eden.
Neville Chamberlain.

Which queen is Cameron a 5th cousin, twice removed, of?

Queen Elizabeth II.

Queen Maxima of the Netherlands.

Queen Letizia of Spain.

Cameron claimed which record from Tony Blair?

The youngest Prime Minister in history.
The most jobs held in civil service before becoming a Prime Minister.
The number of times he attempted to become elected party leader.

He formed a coalition government with the Liberal Democrats in 2010; who was their leader, who also became Cameron's Deputy Prime Minister?

Nick Clegg.
Tim Farron.
Menzies Campbell.

What did this coalition mark?

The first coalition government since World War II.
The first time both Prime Minister and Deputy Prime Minister were from the same extended family.
The first time that the Conservatives found themselves in a coalition.

Why did David Cameron announce his resignation on 24th June 2016?

The public had voted to leave the EU. As he wished to remain in the EU Cameron felt that another Prime Minister should lead "Brexit."
He was exhausted from the exertion of his duties.
His public approval rating was at its highest point since becoming Prime Minister.

Which lady became the next leader of the Conservative Party and the Prime Minister?

Andrea Leadsom.
Theresa May.
Amber Rudd.

What role had she held in Cameron's last government?

Foreign Secretary.
Chancellor of the Exchequer.
Home Secretary.

Who was Theresa May's Foreign Secretary until Summer 2018?

Boris Johnson.
John Major.
Jeremy Hunt.

How much is the Prime Minister's salary per annum, at the time of writing?

£100212.
£151451.
£195643.

Which subject did Theresa May achieve her degree in at St. Hugh's College, Oxford University?

Economics.
Politics.
Geography.

Theresa May's 2017 general election left the country with a coalition government; the second this decade. Who are the Conservatives in a coalition with?

Liberal Democrats.
Plaid Cymru.
Democratic Unionist Party.

What is the name of the 16th century manor house near the village of Ellesborough in Buckinghamshire that every Prime Minister since 1921 has used as a country home?

Diplomacy House.
Chequers Court.
Constitution Cottage.

How many different British Prime Ministers have there been since Queen Elizabeth II's accession in February 1952?

13.
16.
19.

The End. How did you do?

Answers: The 1700's to 1829.

Today, we have the Conservative Party and the Labour Party as Britain's two main political factions vying for votes. Which two parties were operating in the 1700's?

Whig and Tory.

Both party names were originally used by people as insulting terms. Whig was short for *whiggamor,* a Scottish word. What was a whiggamor?

Cattle driver.

What was a Tory, from the Irish word *Toraidhe?* Also called Abhorrers, these figures were supporters of King Charles II when he chose to dissolve parliament in 1679 and they abhorred the petitions being signed to recall parliament.

An outlaw or robber.

Who is widely considered to be the first British Prime Minister?

Sir Robert Walpole.

Was the first Prime Minister a Whig or a Tory?

Whig.

Which monarch did Sir Robert Walpole serve as Prime Minister from 1721 until deposed in 1742?

George II.

Sir George Villiers, High Sheriff of Leicestershire (circa 1544-1606) was the father of George Villiers, 1st Duke of Buckingham, a favourite of King James I (VI of Scotland.) Sir George was an ancestor to how many British Prime Ministers, including David Cameron and Sir Winston Churchill?

16.

Who is the longest serving Prime Minister in British history?

Sir Robert Walpole.

Who was the first Prime Minister to live at 10 Downing Street?

Sir Robert Walpole.

In which year did he move in to 10 Downing Street?

1735.

At that time, 10 Downing Street was officially called the residence of the whom – Another title held by the person we call Prime Minister?

First Lord of the Treasury.

The country's 2nd Prime Minister was a Whig named Spencer Compton, Earl of Wilmington. His tenure was short. Why?

He died in office.

To which Member of Parliament, in his own party, was Compton speaking when he said: "Sir, you have a right to speak, but the House has a right to judge whether they will hear you."

Thomas Pelham-Holles, Duke of Newcastle Upon Tyne.

The 3rd British Prime Minister was Henry Pelham, another Whig and an admirer of Walpole's skills. What relation was he to the 4th Prime Minister, Thomas Pelham-Holles, Duke of Newcastle Upon Tyne?

Younger brother.

Why did Henry Pelham's tenure as Prime Minister last just 7 months from August 1743?

Henry died.

Which role had Thomas Pelham-Holles held for over 30 years before his time as Prime Minister began?

Secretary of State.

How many terms did this Duke of Newcastle upon Tyne spend as Prime Minister?

2.

What was Pelham-Holles' nickname?

Hubble-bubble.

Which Prime Minister negotiated peace to end the 1756-1763 pan-European and colonial Seven Years War?

John Stuart, 3rd Earl of Bute.

What role had John Stuart, 3rd Earl of Bute held prior to his selection as the first ever Tory Prime Minister?

Tutor to Prince George, the future King George III.

To decrease national debt, for which drink did Bute introduce a tax in 1763 of 4 shillings per hogshead? The tax caused riots and his resignation from office?

Cider.

His successor, George Grenville, ensured that the above unpopular tax was applied. What else did George Grenville achieve in 1765?

He introduced a stamp tax for mail in the US colonies.

Grenville was dismissed by King George III in 1766. However, the Whigs remained in power under the 2nd Marquess of Rockingham. What was his name?

Charles Watson-Wentworth.

William Pitt the Elder rose to power in 1766; what is he credited with the creation of?

The British Empire.

Which nickname did he earn?

The Great Commoner.

Who did William Pitt the Elder marry on 16th November 1754?

Hester Grenville, future Prime Minister George Grenville's sister.

Scandalous Prime Minister, Augustus Henry Fitzroy, the 3rd Duke of Grafton owed his political survival to what major factor?

His wife Anne's affair, pregnancy by her lover and remarriage post-divorce surpassed his misdemeanours in the electorate's opinion.

Which Tory was Prime Minister when America gained independence from British rule?

Lord Frederick North.

For how many years was this man the Prime Minister of Britain? (Although he is remembered unfavourably as the man who "lost" America.)

12.

Whig Prime Minister William Petty served in 1782-1783. Which aristocratic titles did Petty hold?

2nd Earl of Shelburne. 1ˢᵗ Marquess of Lansdowne.

William Petty's successor said: "My fears are not that the attempt to perform this duty will shorten my life, but that I shall neither bodily nor mentally perform it as I should." Who was he?

William Cavendish-Bentinck, Duke of Portland.

Who delivered the country's first Budget speech in April 1802? The budget was and still is the financial plan of the government laid out in a statement.

Henry Addington, Viscount Sidmouth.

William Pitt the Younger is the youngest Prime Minister in British history. How old was he when he became Prime Minister?

24.

How old was Pitt The Younger when he died?

46.

He oversaw the Act of Union in 1800. What did this act involve?

It united Great Britain with Ireland.

How old was William Pitt the Elder when he passed away in 1778?

69.

Prime Minister Henry Addington's father acted in what capacity to William Pitt the Elder?

Physician.

Which early 19th century Prime Minister said this? "In youth, the absence of pleasure is pain, in old age the absence of pain is pleasure."

Henry Addington, Viscount Sidmouth.

What was Henry Addington's nickname?

The Doctor.

William Wyndham Grenville was the son of George Grenville, Prime Minister 1763-1765. Although William Grenville resigned as Prime Minister in 1807 after only approximately 13 months, what act is he credited with?

The abolition of slavery overseas in the British Empire.

William Grenville was married to which of these ladies?

Anne Pitt, a great niece of William Pitt the Elder.

Between 1809-1812 Spencer Perceval was Tory Prime Minister. What ended his political career?

Assassination.

What career did Perceval pursue prior to politics?

Law.

Who served as British Prime Minister between 1812 and 1827?

Robert Banks-Jenkinson, Earl of Liverpool.

At 119 days, the shortest tenure as Prime Minister is held by George Canning, a former Foreign Secretary. He was Prime Minister between 10th April and 8th August 1827. He believed that "The happiness of constant occupation is infinite." What were his last words as he died of pneumonia?

"Spain and Portugal."

Canning died at Chiswick House in London, owned by successive Dukes of Devonshire until 1929. Which Whig leader passed away at the property in September 1806?

Charles James Fox.

Frederick Robinson, Viscount Goderich was Prime Minister from late 1827 in to 1828. Apart from Goody Goderich and Prosperity Robinson, what was his other nickname?

The Blubberer.

Who became Prime Minister after Viscount Goderich's departure?

Arthur Wellesley, The Duke of Wellington.

Earl Grey passed the 1832 Reform Act which started over a century of further political reforms. What else is Charles Grey renowned for?

A blend of tea.

How many terms did Grey serve as Prime Minister?

1.

In which year did the Tory party become the Conservative party?

1834.

Who was Prime Minister at the time of the name change, confirmed by the Tamworth Manifesto?

Sir Robert Peel.

William IV is reputed to have selected William Lamb, Lord Melbourne to form a government after Earl Grey's resignation because...?

He was the "least bad choice."

How many terms did Lord Melbourne serve as Prime Minister?

2.

Answers: Queen Victoria's Prime Ministers 1837-1901.

Which royal affectionately called Melbourne "Dear Lord M.?"

Queen Victoria.

How old was Arthur Wellesley, The Duke of Wellington when he died in 1852?

83.

What was Wellington's nickname?

The Iron Duke.

Where in London is the Wellington Arch situated?

In Hyde Park.

"There seem to me to be very few facts, at least ascertainable facts, in politics." Which Prime Minister is quoted as saying this?

Sir Robert Peel.

Who was Prime Minister for 3 short tenures; in 1852,1858-1859 and 1866-1868?

Edward Stanley Smith, 14th Earl of Derby.

George Hamilton Gordon, Earl of Aberdeen was Prime Minister 1852-1855, which poet was he related to?

George Byron.

Aberdeen resigned in 1855 because of his perceived failures managing which crisis?

The Crimean War.

Henry Temple, Viscount Palmerston, replaced Aberdeen. In 1857 he was instrumental in which of these matters?

Introducing the divorce court in Britain.

Which of these was one of his nicknames?

Lord Cupid.

Lord John Russell, Prime Minister 1856-1862 and 1866-1867, was the 3rd son of which duke?

6th Duke of Bedford.

In which year was Benjamin Disraeli "Dizzy" born?

1804.

A Prime Minister twice, Disraeli was also an acclaimed what?

Writer.

He is the only British Prime Minister in history to be of which faith?

Judaism.

In which year was Disraeli given the title of Earl of Beaconsfield?

1879.

Why was this earldom awarded, primarily?

He had succeeded in making Queen Victoria the Empress of India.

What was the name of Dizzy's country home located in High Wycombe, Buckinghamshire? Today it is open to the public.

Hughenden Manor.

William Gladstone, Queen Victoria's least favourite Prime Minister, held the position how many times during his political career?

4.

Born in Liverpool in 1809, in which year did Gladstone's last tenure as Prime Minister begin?

1892.

Where in London was Gladstone buried in 1898? (He died on 19th May at Hawarden Castle in Wales.)

Westminster Abbey.

In 1894, the 5th Earl of Rosebery became Prime Minister. What was his name?

Archibald Phillip Primrose.

Which princess of the British royal family did he ask permission to marry?

Princess Victoria, daughter of Edward VII and Queen Alexandra.

Why was Rosebery refused permission?

Edward, Prince of Wales and later King Edward VII was opposed to royals marrying political figures.

Robert Gascoyne-Cecil, 3rd Marquess of Salisbury was created Prime Minister on three separate occasions. Which renowned figure was he a descendant of?

William Cecil, Lord Burghley, Queen Elizabeth I's long serving chief advisor and Secretary of State.

What record does the 3rd Marquess of Salisbury hold amongst Prime Ministers?

He was the tallest Prime Minister in British history.

Which educational establishments did the three Prime Ministers between 1880 and 1902 all attend?

Eton and Christ Church, Oxford University.

Answers: 20th Century Prime Ministers.

In 1900, Winston Churchill, two time 20th century Conservative Prime Minister, first became a Member of Parliament. For which town did he compete in 1899 and lose before a win in 1900?

Oldham.

Arthur Balfour replaced the Marquess of Salisbury as Prime Minister in 1902. What relationship did they have?

Salisbury was Balfour's uncle.

Which renowned philosopher and Prime Minister said: "I am more or less happy when being praised, not very comfortable when being abused, but I have moments of uneasiness when being explained."

Arthur Balfour.

Henry Campbell-Bannerman became Prime Minister in 1905. Why was history made?

It was the first time that the title of Prime Minister was officially used.

He died at 10 Downing Street in 1908. What abbreviation was he normally referred to by?

CB.

Campbell-Bannerman's Chancellor of the Exchequer became the new Prime Minister. Who was he?

Herbert Henry Asquith.

Which Prime Minister is the only one to have served 3 monarchs during their time in office? (George V, Edward VIII and George VI.)

Stanley Baldwin.

In 1925 H.H. Asquith was given the Order of the Garter, the highest chivalric order, and which title?

Earl of Oxford and Asquith.

What financial support measure did Asquith implement in 1909? Payment was subject to meeting criteria; including being of "good character."

The state pension for the over 70's.

Who succeeded Asquith as Prime Minister on 6th December 1916?

David Lloyd George.

H.H. Asquith's son, Anthony, 1902-1968, became known to the public by embracing which profession?

Film directing.

Prime Minister Andrew Bonar Law instigated which of these to help Britain recover from the First World War?

The Tranquillity Manifesto.

How long was Andrew Bonar Law the Prime Minister for?

209 days.

What did David Lloyd George's fall as Prime Minister result in?

The Liberal Party never formed a government again.

Which Conservative Prime Minister had author and journalist Rudyard Kipling as a cousin?

Stanley Baldwin.

In 1943, aged 80, David Lloyd George caused a scandal by doing what?

He married his secretary (and mistress.)

Who was the first Labour Party Prime Minister in 1924?

James Ramsay-McDonald.

Ramsay-McDonald was said to have been infatuated with which society and political hostess?

Edith, Marchioness of Londonderry.

Between 1924-1929, Churchill served in which political office? A colourful character, he had defected to the Liberals in 1904 but returned to the Conservatives (calling himself a Constitutionalist) in the November 1924 general election.

Chancellor of the Exchequer.

How many times did Stanley Baldwin serve as Prime Minister?

3.

Which Conservative Prime Minister was faced with Edward VIII's abdication crisis in 1936? He made it clear that Edward could not marry divorcee Wallis Simpson and remain on the throne; the head of the Church of England. (Edward never forgave him.)

Stanley Baldwin.

Which Prime Minister optimistically, and mistakenly, said: "This is the second time in our history that there has come back from Germany to Downing Street peace with honour. I believe it is peace for our time."

Neville Chamberlain.

What role did Neville Chamberlain hold before he became Prime Minister?

Chancellor of the Exchequer.

Having already won the Nobel Prize for Literature in 1953, what unique honour was bestowed on Sir Winston Churchill by the US Congress on 9th April 1963?

US Citizenship.

Clement Attlee and the Labour Party won the first election after World War II. What organisation did his government create? It was officially launched on 5th July 1948?

The National Health Service.

Churchill and the Conservatives returned to power in 1951. Between October 1951 and early March 1952 Churchill also served in which office? The new holder of the role had to conclude his duties as Governor General of Canada.

Minister of Defence.

Sir Anthony Eden succeeded Winston Churchill as Prime Minister in 1955; which high profile role in government did he hold for 3 separate terms prior to the top job?

Foreign Secretary.

Knighted in 1954, Eden was given which earldom in 1961?

Earl of Avon.

What nickname did Harold MacMillan, the Conservative Prime Minister from 1957-1963, have?

Supermac.

What did MacMillan tell Queen Elizabeth II when he took on the role of Prime Minister?

That he thought his government would last less than 6 weeks.

MacMillan was the last former Prime Minister to be created an Earl in 1984. He became the Earl of Stockton. What rank of honour have later ministers achieved as "life peers?" e.g. Margaret Thatcher and John Major.

Former Prime Ministers have been awarded baronetcies.

Sir Alec Douglas-Home followed Macmillan as Conservative leader and Prime Minister. How long was he Prime Minister for?

363 days.

What was unusual about his appointment as Prime Minister?

He renounced his earldom, and his seat in the House of Lords, to serve as Prime Minister in the House of Commons.

Labour, led by Harold Wilson (1916-1995) won the 1964 election by what majority?

4.

Harold was Wilson's middle name, what was his true first name?

James.

Why did Wilson call a general election in 1970?

He was confident that he, and the Labour Party, would win resoundingly.

Who became the Prime Minister after the 1970 election?

Edward Heath.

What political role did Wilson hold between 1974-1976?

Prime Minister.

Which Prime Minister suspended the Death Penalty in England, Wales and Scotland?

Harold Wilson.

What was unique about James Callaghan's career?

He was the only 20th century Prime Minister to have held the 4 major offices (Prime Minister, Chancellor, Home Secretary and Foreign Secretary.)

What rank did Edward Heath achieve in the British army during the Second World War?

Lieutenant-Colonel.

Despite both being Conservatives, which future Prime Minister was Heath a high-profile critic of?

Margaret Thatcher.

During Callaghan's tenure, how high did unemployment rise?

1.5 million people.

The May 1979 general election was won by which leader and party?

Margaret Thatcher, Conservatives.

Who was the longest serving 20th century British Prime Minister?

Margaret Thatcher.

When Margaret Thatcher became Conservative Prime Minister, she was the first female Prime Minister in British history. How many females have filled this role since?

1.

Margaret Thatcher's father, Alfred Roberts, had filled which office in Grantham, Lincolnshire?

Mayor.

What was Margaret Thatcher's nickname?

The Iron Lady.

What was a major factor in her downfall as Prime Minister?

The introduction of the Poll Tax.

During the 1990's the Labour Party, led by Tony Blair, rebranded as New Labour. They were said to be influenced by which iconic Prime Minister's visions?

Margaret Thatcher.

Who succeeded Thatcher as Prime Minister on 28th November 1990, holding the office until 2nd May 1997?

John Major.

What major role had this man held in Thatcher's last government?

Chancellor of the Exchequer.

At what age did John Major win his first seat as a Conservative councillor for Lambeth Council in London? (Born 1943.)

21.

He won his first parliamentary seat – Huntingdon in Cambridgeshire - in which year?

1979.

Answers: Recent History.

Former Labour Prime Minister Gordon Brown holds a doctorate in which subject from Edinburgh University?

History.

Gordon is his middle name, what is his true Christian name?

James.

Following Princess Diana's death in 1997, which former Prime Minister was appointed as a special guardian to Princes William and Harry?

John Major.

Which party was Tony Blair leader of, and later Prime Minister for, from 1994?

Labour.

What did Blair announce on 27th June 2007?

His resignation as Prime Minister.

Blair was the youngest Prime Minister since Lord Liverpool in 1812. How old was Tony Blair when he became Prime Minister?

43.

Who succeeded Tony Blair, as part of a private deal they had probably agreed in 1994?

Gordon Brown.

What are former Conservative Prime Minister David Cameron's middle names?

William Donald.

Which Conservative politician from Sir Winston Churchill's era is David Cameron related to? You can see the resemblance.

Sir Alfred Duff Cooper.

Which queen is he a 5th cousin, twice removed, of?

Queen Elizabeth II.

Cameron claimed which record from Tony Blair?

The youngest Prime Minister in history.

He formed a coalition government with the Liberal Democrats in 2010; who was their leader, who also became Cameron's Deputy Prime Minister?

Nick Clegg.

What did this coalition mark?

The first coalition government since World War II.

Why did David Cameron announce his resignation on 24th June 2016?

The public had voted to leave the EU. As he wished to remain in the EU Cameron felt that another Prime Minister should lead "Brexit."

Which lady became the next leader of the Conservative Party and the Prime Minister?

Theresa May.

What role had she held in Cameron's last government?

Home Secretary.

How much is the Prime Minister's salary per annum, at the time of writing?

£151451.

Which subject did Theresa May achieve her degree in at St. Hugh's College, Oxford University?

Geography.

Who was Theresa May's Foreign Secretary until Summer 2018?

Boris Johnson.

Theresa May's 2017 general election left the country with a coalition government; the second this decade. Who are the Conservatives in a coalition with?

Democratic Unionist Party.

What is the name of the 16th century manor house near the village of Ellesborough in Buckinghamshire that every Prime Minister has used as a country home since 1921?

Chequers Court.

How many different British Prime Ministers have there been since Queen Elizabeth II's accession in February 1952?

13.

Thanks for reading. Hope you did well. If not, back to the start!

Printed in Great Britain
by Amazon